$\mathcal{T}$he
REDNECK
CHRONICLES

A Country Boy Can Survive

JAMES D. BURLESON, DDS
8/12/2015

This collection of stories traces the progression of Dr. Jim Burleson's "quest for success" including many adventures and misadventures along the way. It also unequivocally verifies his redneck credentials.

Xulon
PRESS

The Redneck Chronicles

This is dedicated to Melba, Marsha, Beth, Stella, Marianna, Bonnie, Desha, Susie, Tricia, Shelley, Ruth, Rachel, Alicia, Dorothy, Nathalia, Sherry and Adelyn (my granddaughter), and all the other amazing women who have enriched my life beyond measure.

Author Acknowledgements

I have known Dr. James Burleson since high school. He is an honest and trustworthy person. His reputation in the community is well-known and he believes in the good of his community and country. He is caring of his patients, employees and friends. He is a good friend and a wonderful person to work with.
–Ruth James

James Burleson is one of the most compassionate and loving men I have ever met. His kindness is unlike any I have ever encountered. He puts others needs before his own and his wife is the love of his life. He is a quiet man but listens intently to those around him. He is one of the best story tellers I have ever heard. I could listen to him speak all day. –Sherry Clements

Dr. James Burleson is not a man of many words but when he does speak, you want to listen because it is either absolutely brilliant or extremely hilarious! I have been in tears with laughter hearing some of his stories. It is a joy to assist him with dentistry daily. –Alicia Sammis

Dr. James is one of the funniest people I know. He always has the best stories to tell and is very knowledgeable in every category. But the one thing that stands out the most about him is how he takes time out of his day to invest in others' lives or just to stop and ask them how they are doing. He has a genuine heart. – Kasey Lemmons

I have gotten the great opportunity of getting to know Dr. James Burleson by getting to assist him at work. Dr. James is one of the most kind and patient men I know. Just seeing his face light up when he tells his stories makes my day. He has a smile that lights up the world. I consider myself blessed getting to know this man and getting to work with him on a daily basis. –Brittany Eversoll

Dr. James Burleson has been my friend for over thirty years, seventeen of which, he has been my employer. A great storyteller has now become a great writer of these stories his staff and friends loved to hear him tell. –Bonnie Vaught

I had the honor of working with Dr. James Burleson for several years and will always consider him a dear friend. I always looked forward to hearing his stories during our lunch breaks. Sometimes I would laugh so hard that tears would roll down my face. He will never know how much he influenced my life and I'm so humbled he let me be part of his life. –Shelley Williams

I am so thankful to have been a part of Dr. Burleson's dental practice for many years. The stories he would tell us were amazing, funny and sometimes made us cry. He was like the "Father" I never had. He is such a caring, kind-hearted person and I feel so blessed to call him not only a prior boss but a life-long friend. –Tricia Hedrick

Table of Contents

Chapter 1

The Great Pumpkin Enterprise

Among his many endeavors my grandfather had a steam-powered sawmill. The last time he moved the mill he left behind a huge mountain of sawdust about an eighth of a mile from our house. When I was seven I discovered the house-sized abandoned mountain, now decayed into a potting soil texture. I asked my father if I could plant pumpkins there. "What'll you do with pumpkins?" he asked. "Sell them," I replied.

The next spring, when I was eight, my father helped me clear off the vines and other growth on the sawdust pile. I had dried the seeds from my previous Halloween pumpkin and I was determined to plant them all. Starting at the top, I planted seeds on the entire mountain, along with a few cantaloupes and watermelons. I paid little attention to the multitude of snakeskins on the mountain—the snakes really loved that sawdust.

Every week that summer I'd take my hoe and walk barefoot to weed my pumpkin patch. The soil was loose and easy to hoe and smelled very earthy and rich. We had sufficient rainfall that summer and by early October I had a mountain full of pump-kins. We didn't own a truck, so Dad and I took a tractor and small trailer to bring the pumpkins to our house. Only then did I realize how many large pumpkins I had.

We didn't have a telephone back then, so I had to wait until the next time we went to the town of Carlisle to stop by my Uncle Doyle's house to see if he would haul my pumpkins to the produce market in Little Rock. Early the next Saturday Uncle Doyle and my dad built sideboards for his truck so we could haul all the pumpkins in one load, thereby not wasting any fif-teen-cents-a-gallon gasoline. I had weighed some of the pump-kins on our cotton scales and counted them as we loaded them, so I knew pretty much what the load weighed. We set out for Little Rock with Uncle Doyle driving, Dad on my right, and me in the middle trying to dodge the floor-mounted gearshift. We drove very slowly and arrived around noon.

I wasn't impressed with the first buyer. He was heavy-set, chewed tobacco and wouldn't even get out of his chair to look at my pumpkins. "I'll give you $25.00 for the load," he drawled. "No thank you, sir," I replied. The next buyer was more accommodating and offered me seven cents a pound for the load. I quickly did the math and accepted his offer. He was surprised as the scales neared the eight hundred pound mark, but he reached into his pocket and pulled out $53.00 in cash. After giving Uncle Doyle $10.00, I pocketed the balance . I bought a pair of school shoes and purchased a single shot .22 rifle from the Sears catalog ($9.99 plus S&H). That rifle served me well on many hunting adventures and I recently refinished the well-worn stock to pass on to my grandchildren.

I put the remaining money into safe-keeping, hoping to someday buy my own bicycle. There were three of us kids and money was scarce, so we had to share one bicycle. The one I really longed for was $49.00 (plus S&H) in the Sears catalog. I tried for years to save up that much money, but necessities always drained my resources. I never did get that bike, but I did get an important life lesson: we don't always get what we want and it usually turns out for the best. There is a great difference between a want and a need.

Chapter 2

Uncle John Saves the Church

Hebron Methodist Church is located in the farming community of Wattensaw south of Hickory Plains. The congregation was an aggregate of God-fearing hardworking very conservative folk, especially Brother Dave a church deacon. He was consistently and adamantly against any idea that involved change. Upon broaching the subject he would become agitated; his eyes blinking and his chubby cheeks and lips moving like a gigantic grasshopper. The sanctuary's only heat source was a large pot-bellied wood-burning stove with a long chimney pipe reaching up through the attic and roof. The church folk, especially the women, were tired of cleaning up ashes, bark and dirt from the stove, but Brother Dave had stymied its removal.

On one very cold January morning most of the parishioners sat up front near the heat source. Brother Martin, the pastor, was delivering a very energetic hell-fire-and-brimstone sermon. The stove was roaring with the dampers wide open.

Suddenly a different roar began emanating from the attic and smoke began filtering into the sanctuary. "Fire!" someone yelled. My father, a genius of improvisation, directed the men to stand up a long church pew against the back wall to serve as a make-shift ladder. My very athletic Uncle John D., dressed in his best (and only) suit, volunteered to scale the ladder. Upon reaching the top he head-butted out one of the ceiling panels and pulled himself into the attic. He leapt from rafter to rafter, and soon the sounds of flailing and coughing were heard from the vicinity of the stovepipe as John beat out the fire.

He lowered himself onto the pew and slid down to the floor as the congregation applauded. Everyone had been so enthralled with the drama unfolding that no one had evacuated. John was soot-black from head to toe and still clutched the charred remnant of his suit coat. The dampers on the stove had been quickly closed to smother the fire. That stove was never to be used again. By the next Sunday, new propane heaters had been installed and the wood burner was gone. Brother Dave never said a word.

Chapter 3

The Coon Seekers

In the early years before animals had rights and most everyone I knew dreamed of rising to what is now called the poverty level, coon pelts were the golden fleeces I and my boyhood Argonauts sought. This quest offered adventure and great riches: $6.00 for a prime pelt. My mentor was one of the great unheralded woodsmen of our time, Espie Rogers. He was an encyclopedia of everything that crawled, slithered, ran, flew or turned green in the spring. He could move through the woods like an Indian.

I'd be sitting under a tree as still as a nine-year-old could be, perfectly attuned to my surroundings while watching and listening for the slightest sound or movement. Suddenly he would be standing next to me. "Ya doin any good?" he'd ask, as I jumped out of my skin and then pretended to know he was there all the time. "No, not much," I'd say as I surveyed the squirrel tails or feathers protruding from his hunting vest. He could look at a track in the mud and tell what critter had made it, when, where it was going, and what it was going to do when it got there. Espie had an unnerving way of killing snakes. He'd grab them by the tail—copperhead, cottonmouth or whatever, pop them like a whip and release them in one quick motion. The snakes wouldn't even twitch. "Never been bit," he'd say matter-of-factly.

My brother Stan and I frequently followed Espie on his forays in the creek bottoms and picked up lots of valuable lore about hunting and trapping. Espie always seemed to get whatever he was after. I soon learned every footlog, den tree and slough on Collins Creek and Wattensaw Bayou. Using my blackberry-picking money, I procured six traps from Fulcher's Hardware in Carlisle, to supplement those my father had, and started my own trap line. I'd soaked the traps in stump water to stain and remove scent and done everything I'd been taught to do, but I still wasn't catching much. Espie told me I should wrap the trip pedals with aluminum foil. Coons would see the moon's reflection and would have to check it out. I tried this tactic and could hardly wait to see what would happen.

The next morning was windy and bone-chilling cold. I set out to check my traps about 5:30 a.m., allowing time to get home, do chores, eat breakfast and walk to Highway 13 to catch the school bus. I was wearing three layers of clothes plus my new mail-ordered trapper's boots. I carried a short piece of pipe to dispatch any coons not drowned by my water sets. I didn't want to risk damage to the fur by bullet holes. What I soon encountered exceeded my wildest expectations. Almost every other trap held a coon. I waded through the shore ice and gathered my bounty.

I'd set one trap a bit shallow and the coon it held was not happy. I would advance and get my pipe ready to swing. Then it would snarl and lunge at me and I'd retreat. This standoff continued until my mixed-breed spaniel Tubby (who had followed on the sly) launched off the bank and landed on the coon. In a heartbeat the coon had flipped the small dog and was holding it under water. The events that next transpired can best be described as a lesson in abject stupidity. I waded into the fray trying to kick the coon off the dog. As I kicked, the coon released the dog and latched onto my leg. As I tried to jump back, my unencumbered foot slipped from beneath me and I fell backwards, going completely under water. I came up sputtering and swinging, and soon ended the contest.

As I stuffed the coon in my sack I surveyed the damage. The dog was okay; my ankle and new, mail-ordered boots were not. A pair of ugly gashes ran up the side of my new boot and my leg. I knew the leg would heal. I was more concerned with the boot. I limped home and showed my father the sack of coons and ruined boot. I slipped into the storage shed and poured coal oil on my wound. I knew it worked for snakebite and figured it ought to be good for coon bites as well. I then changed clothes and walked off to meet the bus.

That evening when I walked out the back door to do my chores, there sat my coon-chewed boot, now adorned with a row of overlapping bright red Vulcan patches; the kind you clamped into place and then burned to make it adhere. Hallelujah! I was back in business. The coons had gotten wise to the aluminum foil trick and I never equaled that initial catch, but I did wear those boots for some years to come. As I got older my interest turned to coon-hunting with dogs. I'd purchased a Sears and Roebuck single-shot rifle with open sights and a maple stock for the princely sum of $9.99 (plus shipping and handling).

I struck up a friendship with Don Williams (nicknamed Charlie), a boy my own age who lived across the bayou and rode the same school bus. He had some really good multi-purpose fox-deer-coon hounds. In those days we hunted with carbide lamps mounted on our hats with metal strips cut from Folgers coffee cans. The flashlight was saved for use only after the coon was treed. We had no telephone so arrangements were made at school beforehand.

I'd set off with my rifle, gunnysack, carbide light and my bright red Vulcan-patched boots to whatever rendezvous point we'd pre-determined. He'd always be there with the dogs, his hunting knife and revolver stuck in his belt in case close combat became necessary. If the dogs had already struck a hot trail I'd just walk to the sound of the chase. We'd spend most of the night wading through mud, barbed wire and sawbriars, and would often do quite well.

On one occasion while hunting on Wattensaw, Charlie's hounds ran a coon up an exceptionally tall black gum tree. Charlie stood behind me with the flashlight and when it reflected on the coon's eyes I squeezed off a shot. Out rolled the coon—thud!

Congratulations were in order as we examined the bullet hole right between the eyes. I'd forgotten the gunnysack, so we opened the game pouch on Charlie's jacket (which buttoned inside) and stuffed the large coon inside. With some difficulty Charlie put his jacket back on and we resumed our quest. We'd walked maybe a quarter-mile when pandemonium erupted.

"Expletive! Expletive!" yelled Charlie, as he tore off his coat and threw it in the leaves. (He'd learned those words from a hired hand.) Gunfire erupted as Charlie drew his pistol and fired point blank into the now moving coat. "I felt his paws working up my backbone!" Charlie related, with a slight quaver in his voice. Closer inspection of the now expired coon revealed what had happened. My .22 short had struck between the eyes all right but had just broken the skin. It traveled up the slope of the skull and exited between the ears. I'd merely cold-cocked him. When he revived inside the coat he started groping with his paws, causing the aforementioned fracas.

After verifying the coon's demise, Charlie donned his still-smoking jacket and we set off after the dogs which were now on a hot trail. Twenty minutes later, a coon was treed up a lightening-lopped cypress in the middle of the bayou. Fearing for the safety of his dogs in the deep water (and because I had the rifle and could shoot from the bank), Charlie disrobed and waded into the chilly waist-deep water where his dogs were baying and swimming around the tree. Those hounds were really pumped! Clad only in his underwear and carbide-lamp cap, with his teeth chattering and skin turning blue, Charlie yelled, "Knock him out!" I did, and the coon fell into the water.

Charlie reached it first and whooped, as he held the coon over his head. Big mistake! He now became the tree the coon was in, and four very eager hounds were climbing him to get to the coon. "AAAAAARRRRRRRGGGGGGGHHHH!" echoed through the swamp as Charlie heaved the coon as far as he could. He looked as if he'd just lost a bear fight. The cold water soon stopped the bleeding and he waded back out to reclaim the coon after the dogs were satisfied it was dead. Coons are remarkably durable; the hide was still in saleable condition. Since it was almost sunup and we had chores to do we called it a night.

As Charlie and I grew older and were allowed to drive (we learned to drive real young back then), our hunting range increased tremendously. I drove an ancient black F-100 Ford pickup with a flathead V-8 but no second gear, and Charlie drove a slightly new white Chevrolet. Our fathers never put much stock in mud-grip tires, and since most of our destinations were beyond the road's end, we usually took both trucks and a chain to pull each other out of "soft spots".

One particular night we met on the upper end of Faras Run Creek north of Carlisle. We set off with the dogs but soon discovered neither of us had brought matches for our carbide lamps. We pressed on anyway, stumbling through sloughs and briars. Then we hit upon the idea of lighting the lamps with the muzzle flash from the pistol. We fired almost all our rounds with the lamp valves open, but to no avail. The gunfire, however, did cause the coyotes to start howling—lots of coyotes; they closed in on us from three sides. The dogs got spooked and came in, trying to walk between our legs. We decided to retreat and set out for the truck.

On another night my younger brother Stan, our friendTim McCallie and I decided to hunt the Indian burial mounds on Tim's dad's farm on the bayou. My brother carried his $11.99 model, J.C. Penney, single-shot .22 rifle. We took him along because he could always shoot better than we could, even though he was a lot younger. It was early in the season and was still warm enough for snakes. We were just a little spooked by the ambient "spirits" as we climbed the tallest of the heavily timbered mounds.

The dogs had yet to strike and I just turned to say something to Tim when a huge fireball descended on us, turning the night to day. A noise like a squadron of jets almost knocked us flat. Tim yelled and fell on his back, emptying his rifle at the "thing". After we had all finished jumping and hollering, we decided that either the spirits had conspired to scare the hell out of us or we had almost been struck by a meteorite. It was probably a meteorite since smoke was descending upon us. We never found a crater so we surmised it must have burned out just before it struck.

We had many more adventures and misadventures, but we began discovering girls and the coon quests became less frequent. It

seems we all became more civilized and took on socially accept-
able pursuits, then went our separate ways.

Those days of youthful enthusiasm and boundless energy are
long gone. I hope there will always be wild places, coonhounds
and boys to enjoy them. Looking back, I wouldn't have had it
any other way.

Chapter 4

The Bayou

I'm old enough to remember when Wattensaw Bayou ran clear year-round. The contiguous green belt of trees and the resulting humus layer collected and dispensed water as needed during flood or drought: that's what God intended. I remember catching lots of catfish, bass, crappie, bream and the occasional tackle-busting grinnel. We didn't cull any species. I still remember the sweet cottony texture of those grinnel.

Dad, Stan and I would don long pants and boots and wade into the flowing water, working our way upstream. We used cane poles and fished slowly to avoid spooking the fish, giving the cottonmouths a wide berth .

As we caught fish, we'd put them on stringers attached to our belts, checking often to prevent snapping turtles from eating our fish. The long pants were to keep the leeches off. Invariably a few would always latch on and were uncomfortable to remove, but this was a small price to pay.

Today most of the bayou has been denuded of its forest, pumped dry for irrigation, and fouled by livestock operations.

On the bayou or any outdoor setting it's imperative to be aware of your surroundings. Once as I returned from a squirrel hunt I was walking a beaver dam to cross the bayou. I started noticing different colored wires sticking out of the dam and realized it had been rigged with dynamite! I started yelling and running. Upon clearing the north bank I saw two men stringing wire and preparing to detonate. A kid crossing their explosives was the last thing they'd expected. If I'd been just a little slower my story would have ended then and there.

I hunted and fished a good bit of the bayou, but there was a long stretch above Collins Creek that I wanted to explore. When we were still quite young, Stan and I convinced our dad to allow a hunting float trip from the Highway 13 Bridge to Espie Rogers' farm. We had a heavy flat-bottomed boat and no motor, so we were paddle-powered and would float with the current. One warm Saturday in November, Stan and I loaded the boat into our pickup and Dad drove us to the drop point. I'd timed the float to coincide with high water. The bayou was over its banks and flowing fast. Piece of cake, I thought. This should be an easy float. We loaded paddles, guns, shells and a water jug into the boat, and slid it down the embankment into the swirling flood. Stan was in front with his single-shot 12 Gauge Iver-Johnson. He was a good shot and generally killed more with that gun than I did with my Remington 1100. We were mostly after ducks and squirrels on this trip.

The first hour went as planned. We were seeing lots of squirrels, but had to time our shots so they fell on dry land or shallow water so the squirrels wouldn't sink and get lost. Stan had made a couple of nice shots at flushing ducks and we had three squirrels in the boat. We'd noticed a dark cloud back to the west and the wind began to pick up. We'd dressed in warm-weather clothes and I hadn't listened to the weather forecast- they were pretty much worthless back then. We quit hunting and started paddling like crazy, as the wind started shearing limbs off the trees above us. We tried to dodge, but were getting thumped pretty well by falling debris.

We were about a mile above Collins Creek when Armageddon happened. Bill McCallie had bulldozed all the trees on the south side of the bayou and many had fallen into the waterway, blocking the channel. We'd navigate where we could then drag that heavy boat around the fallen trees. We rigged a rope harness to the boat and must have looked like a pair of mules in overdrive, heaving and dragging the boat. About the time we cleared the debris field the icy rain began coming down in sheets. We were filthy, cold, wet and tired. The wind shrieked, trees and limbs broke, and the lightning intensified. We paddled like madmen and covered the last stretch in record time.

As we neared the takeout point we decided to take refuge under a high-cut bank, as we thought this might offer some protection. We tied off the boat and slid under the overhang. That's when we got to experience a lightning strike firsthand. A brilliant flash engulfed us. A large cypress not ten paces away exploded, covering us with bark and mud. The violence was indescribable. We were temporarily stunned and couldn't hear anything, but we were <u>very</u> lucky to be alive. We would come back for the boat the next day. We grabbed our guns and game and walked home with the lightning still popping. We just figured it was not our day to die. In retrospect, wearing rubber boots and standing on dry ground saved us. My left ear never recovered from the thunderbolt.

Chapter 5

The Bull Rider

My father had always raised Hereford cattle; but they are less resistant to certain diseases than other breeds. When I was about ten, he swapped our Hereford bull for a young Angus to improve the herd's disease resistance.

My first up-close-and-personal encounter with the new bull occurred the next spring. One of our cows was not doing well, and my father told me to take her a bucket of "sweet feed" and to keep the other cattle away while she fed. The young Angus bull smelled the feed and developed a hankering for it. I swatted him with my stick and thought I'd deterred him. I had my back to him when I heard him stomp. I turned toward him just in time for him to plant his big head in my midsection. The impact carried me backwards and I landed hard on my back, with the bucket of feed spilling over my head. That's when I named him Satan. He walked forward and straddled me while he ate the feed. I was totally knocked breathless from the head-butt and the impact with the ground and couldn't move. Worse, I was left staring directly up at his bull-parts; I sure hoped he wouldn't add insult to injury. It took an eternity for him to finish eating and stroll away, and he (thankfully) didn't step on me. With wounded pride and bruised ribs, I gathered my empty bucket and limped home.

My next encounter with Satan came when he needed his shots. He was now full-grown and very big. My dad had put a nose-clamp on Satan, which was attached to a strong rope. He and the bull were on one side of the woven wire fence while I was on the other. He cinched the rope three times around a very sturdy cross-tie fence post and passed the free end to me. "Hold tight and don't let the rope slip!" he yelled. I was so nervous I almost wet myself-that bull was huge. I had a premonition that I was about to die, and with good reason. When Dad plunged the syringe into Satan he bellowed and went berserk. I was pulling as hard as I could but the rope was slipping; my knuckles were almost into the fence. When Satan had enough slack, he threw his head up, kicked hard with his back legs and flipped com-pletely upside down over the fence, landing on his back where I had been standing seconds before. Fortunately I had turned the rope loose. Otherwise he would have probably broken his neck. My dad didn't see it that way and I got all the blame.

Before I became interested in bull riding I tried my hand at horseracing. My good friend Don Northcutt had set up a "race-track" in his pasture. To get to the finish line we had to skirt around a large post oak tree with lots of protruding roots while simultaneously ducking low to avoid the limbs overhead. The horses had to be dragged to the starting line but were very eager to get back to the barn (finish line) and would run like thoroughbreds. One particular day, I was riding a jug-head gelding that had been mad at the world since he'd been "fixed". I was behind in the race and tried to make up time by cutting close to the tree. I grabbed the saddle horn and leaned far left to get under the limb. When I did, my cinch straps gave way and the saddle, with me on it, slipped under the horse's belly. I fell off, got horse stomped and slid into the tree roots, injuring my knee. I didn't know that I'd torn my ACL—this would be a lifetime injury and would reoccur when I tried to play football. I'd also cracked a couple of ribs but I never told my parents or went to the doctor. It really hurt to breathe for the next couple of weeks.

On another occasion, that same horse inadvertently introduced me to saddle-bronc riding. Don and I were riding one hot summer day when we decided to let the horses drink from his stock pond. It was snaky, scummy and choked with button-willows. Of course, my gelding decided to go swimming and waded into the deep water. That's where things got interesting. Don yelled, "Wasps!" Just to the left of my horse's head was a red wasp nest as large as a sunflower. I yanked the reins hard to the right but true to his contrary nature, my mount lunged left into the nest prompting an immediate mass attack.

He snorted, swung his head and began a series of stiff-legged jumps followed by a bucking frenzy. I couldn't see any future in staying on. I got free of the stirrups and did a back layout dive off his left flank. I barely avoided his back hooves and he did a circle kick and tore out across the pasture. I also made haste to get out of dodge. Miraculously, I wasn't injured or even stung. It took a while to catch the horse—he obviously blamed me for the whole ordeal. I'd no sooner grabbed the reins when he reached out and bit me hard on the right shoulder. I learned never to turn my back on a pissed-off horse.

After horseracing, for some reason I had become obsessed with bull riding. I'd been to the Lonoke rodeo and thought I knew the basics. I started riding yearling calves, holding tight to the mane while kicking my legs and waving my free hand. I also knew to lean backward to absorb the force. Gosh, I'm getting good, I thought, but I had my sights set on the ultimate challenge – Satan!

I picked a time when I knew my dad would be gone for a good while. It was a cold January day and the feedlot was covered with a foot of soft, wet manure. I hastily built my "chute" out of oak gates leaving it open on both ends. I put out a bucket of sweet feed (he still loved it) and guided him in. I climbed on to the chute and hovered over his back. That's when things really got stupid. I yelled and dropped onto his back, moving my arm and kicking my legs. I hadn't noticed that he had no mane— there was nothing to hold onto! He bellowed and charged out of the chute. Miraculously, I stayed on until he started to buck. I panicked and leaned forward. He launched me skyward and I did a 1 ¼ back flip, landing on my back and shoulders and getting buried deep in the soft manure.

Words cannot describe the power of a mature bull; you have to experience it. His backbone was so hard it felt like having your backside pounded by a cinder block. Satan was still bucking and snorting as my brother Stan helped dig me out of the manure. Satan wasn't a mean bull; otherwise he would have come over and stomped me. I certainly couldn't go to the house in my condition so I went to our nearby reservoir and "fell in". It took a while to get the manure off. That water was cold! I was blue, shivering and hypothermic by the time I reached the house, but never did tell my parents. I lost all interest in bull riding.

Chapter 6

Johnnie's First Deer

Before he was a naval officer, Golden Gloves boxer and exceptional dentist, John Butler and his brother Jimmy were raised in a single-parent home; they were quite a handful for their schoolteacher mom, Elsie.

This particular story was related by John's Uncle Warren. Warren's middle name was Elmer, hence his nickname "Uncle Fudd". Warren became John's mentor after John's father died at a young age. He introduced him to hunting and took him to his first deer camp. Against Warren's advice, young Johnnie spent the entire night exercising his considerable skill at poker and emptying everyone else's wallets.

Shortly before shooting light, Warren guided John to his deer stand–a piece of plywood nailed between two limbs high in an oak tree. John promptly fell asleep but not before tying a rope between his belt and the tree, as instructed. Warren took a stand nearby so he could monitor his young protégé. Sometime later, John was awakened from a deep slumber by a sound he'd never heard before. As he collected his wits he saw a large buck snorting and pawing the ground. Apparently, John had relieved himself before climbing the tree and the buck had taken offense.

John raised his rifle, fired and dropped the deer. He was in such a hurry to check out his first deer that he jumped from his stand, aiming to land on a brush pile at the base of the tree. In his haste, however, he forgot about the rope tethering him to the tree. As he leapt, the rope snapped tight and jerked him upside down, slamming him against the tree trunk and almost ripping his pants off. Dazed, John grabbed the rope and pulled himself upright with the rope pulling his pants way up, giving him a very painful wedgie.

In anguish and not thinking clearly, John whipped out his new hunting knife and severed the rope. He bounced off a couple of limbs like a shot-gunned squirrel and landed fortunately on the brush pile. Warren, having witnessed the entire debacle ran quickly to the brush pile and determined that there were no serious injuries. He smiled and said, "Johnnie, in all my years of hunting I've never seen anything like that. Are you ready for a rematch? Because right now, the deer looks considerably better than you do!" Uncle Fudd had nailed it.

Chapter 7

The Blizzard

Years later, I had reason to be thankful that John's survival skills had greatly improved. John, Jimmy, his Mormon friend and I were mule deer hunting high in the Utah Mountains. The weather was unusually hot even at that high altitude. We'd made camp on a wide open plateau to take advantage of the wind currents for cooling purposes. Earlier in the day, we'd killed two mule deer. We sent Jimmy and our guide back down the mountain in our blazer so the meat wouldn't spoil. This left John and I alone on the mountain with no transportation.

About sunset we noticed dark clouds building toward the west. We'd no sooner crawled into our sleeping bags when the wind picked up and lightning and thunder ensued. Our tent was ripped off of us and literally blown off the mountain. We were now exposed to torrential rain and were soon thoroughly soaked. Then the temperature dropped drastically and we were engulfed in a white-out blizzard. John then made a classic understatement. "Jim, this isn't good. We'd better get smart or we're going to die up here." We dragged our frozen sleeping bags and few remaining supplies into a ravine to get out of the wind. Our icy jumpsuits crunched as we walked. We took stock of our remaining supplies: two deer livers, onions, a dozen eggs, a case of frozen beer, no water and a Coleman stove, with a meager amount of fuel. Building a fire in the blowing snow proved impossible. For the next two days we ate scrambled eggs and mostly raw deer liver and onions. We built a snow cave in the ravine and knew it was above freezing in there because our clothes and beer began to thaw.

The third morning, we heard a car horn in the valley far below. We saw the blazer pushing snow up to the headlights. Our Mormon guide was sitting on the hood, holding a long pole. Occasionally, he'd dismount and feel for the road to keep the blazer out of the ditches. When the vehicle reached us we cleaned up the campsite and packed it all in the blazer for the agonizing trip back to Ogden. Miraculously, we had no signs of frostbite.

Chapter 8

The Snake Pit

My wife Melba and I went cane-pole fishing on a private reservoir north of Carlisle. We opted to use my Alumaweld bass boat, since its additional freeboard gave us a false sense of security when it came to snakes. I share Indiana Jones' sentiments on snakes, based on my two-week stay in the Stuttgart Hospital after being bitten by a rattlesnake.

Launching the bigger boat involved wading out to get the boat off the trailer. After seeing several snakes swimming near the shore, we opted to fish in the middle of the reservoir. After catching and releasing a few fish I noticed a larger-than-average snake swimming our way. I slapped the water with my cane pole to scare it away- bad decision. It raised its head way up, bared its fangs and showed the inside of its cotton-white mouth. This isn't good, I thought. My fifty-horsepower motor was tilted up with the prop barely in the water and offered no help in immediate escape. As the snake advanced, I struck it hard with my pole. This enraged the cottonmouth. It bit my trolling motor and proceeded down the port side, biting at the hull every few feet. I grabbed my short paddle and ran to the stern to try to get between the snake and Melba. As I reached the stern, the psychotic snake had already advanced over the prop and lower unit and was coming aboard. I dropped to one knee and swung the paddle hard. It caught the snake up against the cowling, almost cutting it in half. The disabled snake was still biting at my paddle as I pried it loose from the shaft of the motor. Needless to say, that ended our trip. Henceforth, I will carry my 12 Gauge Autoloader shotgun on all trips. Any serpent getting within thirty feet of the boat will be immediately turned into snake burger.

Chapter 9

The Day the Four-Wheeler Died

The weather was unusually warm for the October muzzle loader season. I'd spent the morning not seeing deer, swatting mosquitos and then getting so bored that I started clearing shooting lanes. Around 10:30 a.m. I quit my stand and started toward the truck on my four-wheeler. I'd crossed the bridge over our duck slough and locked the security chain behind me leaving the four-wheeler running. As I turned, smoke and flames were pouring from under the dash. I frantically started dipping water from the slough with my hat to douse the flames and then used it to beat at the fire. Finally, good sense prevailed. I turned off the key and the fire died. Now I faced a dilemma-the wheeler was a quarter of a mile from the truck with lots of mud and sawbriers in between. I tied my deer-dragging harness to the front brush guard with me being the mule. I couldn't get traction and kept slipping down so I tried pushing. I'd put my shoulder to the task, go a few feet and then redirect the steering. I was wishing I had cut a better trail as the saw briers were doing their thing and I was soon bleeding profusely. It seemed like it took an eternity to reach the truck. I was exhausted and drenched in blood and sweat.

I had another dilemma though; how to load the dead wheeler onto the truck. I'd noticed a deep gulley on a nearby hillside and thought it might be useful to lower the truck so I could push my ATV on. I chained the ATV to the truck and dragged it close. I then carefully backed into the gulley and loaded and secured the ATV. My only remaining obstacle was getting the truck out of the gulley. I figured if I accelerated too fast the truck would flip over backwards. I decided it was time for a real-world application of the college physics courses I'd taken. I eased the front of my Nissan® Titan pickup over the embankment. I hoped that the big 5.6-liter V-8 would be heavy enough to keep the truck at a less than vertical incline. With 4WD engaged, I punched the accelerator and the truck literally leapt out of the gulley — applied physics and dumb luck. This was my "Dukes of Hazzard" moment. I decided to drive directly to a nearby ATV shop since I couldn't unload and reload my dead wheeler. I didn't even stop to clean up and change clothes. I tried to slip in a side door unnoticed since I was dripping sweat, mud, blood and swamp water, while still wearing my burned hat.

The showroom was crowded and all eyes turned toward me-busted! A young mother quickly guided her son out of the front door. The owner, a patient of mine, was shocked. "Doc, are you okay?" he asked. "Yes," I replied, "but my four-wheeler's not." I was ushered to the back of the building and, after a quick assessment, the mechanic told me the mother-board was inciner-ated. "Huh?" I replied. "That's almost what I said when it caught fire. At least I got the first word right." Two weeks later, my ATV was as good as new. In hindsight, I am lucky: no heart attack, heat exhaustion or flipped truck. Did I learn my lesson? No, I'll still do stupid stuff; that's part of the adventure. Incidentally, I still wear the hat.

Chapter 10

And Then There Was Stan...

My brother Stan and I are diametrically opposite. I've always been more serious and work-oriented. He's more of a party animal and good-time seeker but he has the intellect to be an over-achiever. Despite being married and making the thirty mile commute daily by motorcycle to UCA in Conway, he was able to make the grades to be accepted to med school. This was much more difficult than my solitary, more time-efficient approach. We rose from the same humble origins; he now has a very successful medical practice in DeWitt.

In high school, he and classmates Blake Hunt and Stuart McBurnett blazed new trails of mischief and hijinks... not destructive, mind you, just disruptive. Silence was to be broken, rules were to be ignored and the band room became a playroom. This trio contributed greatly to the premature graying of several faculty members at Carlisle High. Stan wouldn't allow me to recount specific occurrences and told me I'd better retain legal counsel if I did so. You'll just have to use your wildest imagination.

Stan and I shared an obsession with hunting, especially bird hunting, and frequently accompanied Espie Rogers on lengthy quail-hunting "rounds". He insisted that his dog Priss sit with us on the front seat of his truck. That was the worst smelling dog I've ever experienced; she smelled dead and rotten. Espie said he'd once tried giving her a bath but it only made her stink more. Stan and I would fight for the window seat so we could hang our heads out to breathe. Priss was an excellent bird dog but I'll never know how she smelled quail over her own stinkiness!

Espie had a unique sense of humor. Once, when we approached a sign that read "Hunting by Permission only", he turned to my brother and I and asked, "Do you mind if I hunt here?" We both gave him permission and we got his permission. Having fulfilled the signs' requirements, we proceeded to hunt.

Over our hunting years Stan and I have been fortunate to own a succession of fine bird dogs. It's a shame our medical and dental ambitions appropriated so much of the time that could have been spent afield. I have hundreds of mental images of unforgettable bird dog moments such as the time our two setters simultaneously pointed in a patch of daffodils overlooking a small pond- it doesn't get any prettier than that. Ted, my friend Larry Adams' setter, once stood up against a sweet gum tree and pointed straight up at a patch of honeysuckle. When I threw a stick, a quail flew out. Ted had treed it! On another hunt, Stan's dog, Pat, was making a long retrieve when she locked into a perfect point, while holding the first bird in her mouth. Unbelievable! The quail are now long gone, and all those fine dogs are now long dead, except for the memories.

When I left for dental school Stan gave me one of the most thoughtful gifts possible. He bought and installed seat belts in my Dodge®Polara. He knew I would need all the protection I could get.

Stan has hunted and fished in many parts of the world, from whitewings in Patagonia to ptarmigan in Alaska. He has a beautiful trout lodge on Cow Shoals on the Little Red River and has become a master at fly-fishing, fly-tying and all things trout. If not for him I would never have experienced that world.

In addition to his membership in the McCullum Hunting Club on Big Island (to be covered later), Stan has extensive agricultural holdings and a very large hunting/fishing preserve on Lagrue Bayou near Ethel. His cabin was once a bar room where at least three homicides occurred. After the authorities shut it down he had it moved to his property. A fireplace was installed in one end and the interior was finished with boards cut from huge cypress logs that had been on the bottom of the White River for nearly a century. The walls are now lined with trophy whitetail mounts he has taken from the property. He's an expert marksman and wing-shot; three hundred-plus yard shots are no big challenge. He presented me with a .270 Browning, x-bolt rifle with a Zeiss 3-9x40 scope, which is one sweet shooting, low recoil, very accurate rifle! I love my Remington guns but the Browning is now my long-range weapon of choice. I'm three for three on whitetails including a mid-air shot on an eight-point jumping over my shooting lane.

We share certain similarities: we both chose very demanding healthcare professions, we are both devotees of Gary Larson and The Far Side, and consider him to be one of the great comic geniuses of all time. We also share a distain for liberal politicians and their socialist garbage. We both fought long and hard against insurmountable obstacles to achieve success and have little regard for those who are too lazy to get off their butts to work to better themselves. We are tired of supporting them. We both acquired farmland as soon as finances permitted and our mutual favorite movie is "Jeremiah Johnson".

We both relish the bite of a brisk north wind on a frosty morning, the sting of sleet, snow and freezing rain, squirrels cutting hickory nuts, the aerobatics of mallards descending into green timber, breaking ice as our duck boat races the dawn to reach our designated shooting hole, the adrenaline rush at the appearance of a huge buck slipping through the forest at first light, the cacophony of wild geese, and elk bugling in a misty mountain meadow. We've both spent more time up in a tree (stand) than most monkeys. We've both experienced a thousand unique sunrises that late risers and non-hunters miss. Obviously, we both inherited the same redneck gene. I'm very proud of Stan and all that he's accomplished.

Chapter 11

Big Island

Between the Arkansas and Mississippi Rivers lies one of God's great creations: Big Island. If it weren't for the clouds of mosquitos this would be paradise. It supports an abundance of squirrels, turkeys, deer and bears. The McCullum Hunting Club on Big Island was founded by men who sought the ultimate hunting experience. Early hunters anchored houseboats near the island and used them as a base of operations. In 1951, one of the houseboats and another barge used to transport mules were dismantled and the lumber was used to build the McCullum hunting lodge. Walking a hundred yards from the lodge equates to being transported back in time; everything is green, wild and unspoiled. The club owns one hundred and sixty acres and leases a large tract from Andreson-Tully Timber Company.

My introduction to Big Island came when Stan (a new member) invited me for a weekend squirrel hunt. The river was high so the only way to get there was by boat. We were hauling our gear up the river bank when Stan spotted a skunk nearing the lodge.

Suspecting it might be rabid, he retrieved his rifle and fired a hurried shot as it ran beneath the structure. Unfortunately, the shot was not immediately lethal. That skunk ran under the floor and sprayed and sprayed until it expired. Stan has had extensive nose surgery and can't smell anything. He slept peacefully that night. I, on the other hand, got to enjoy the full force of that odor as it wafted up through the floorboards.

Soon it began to rain. With that symphony playing on the tin roof it was impossible not to sleep. There was no electricity and all power came from a large generator. The cook stove and refrigerator were powered by propane. When that generator was shut off the night became very dark and quiet. The only sounds were the owls, coyotes and the tugboats pushing barges on the river. It was a surreal experience. There's a covered area for skinning and dressing deer, another for scalding and cleaning turkeys and a fish cleaning area. There's a large fire pit with an ancient "liar's log" perfect for recounting the day's hunt, sipping beer and passing the bottle—after the hunt, of course.

The lodge was built on piers six feet above the ground to preclude flooding. No one could have predicted the massive flood of 2011 when water reached seven feet inside the lodge destroying irreplaceable pictures and artifacts and necessitating an extensive rebuilding project. Just upstream from the lodge is a large gravestone marking the final resting place of a river boat captain named Cumby. He was originally interred on another riverbank, but as it eroded, his tombstone was in peril of falling into the river. Using a very large boat, club members under the direction of a coroner carefully toppled the gravestone on to the deck and moved his remains and monument to its current location.

Back to the squirrel hunt. There was something very special about old growth forest. The trees were immense. The pecan trees we hunted were so tall that squirrels feeding in the tree-tops were out of range of shotguns—honest—so we had to use rifles. I had a very good morning. Using my very accurate 552 Remington auto loader, I fired fourteen shells to get my limit of 8-four grays and four blacks. These were very long shots.

During my explorations, I discovered a massive sycamore tree. It was over twenty feet in circumference at chest height and one hundred feet tall. I used a compass and geometric formula to measure the height. The trunk and massive limbs were a striking iridescent white and glowed like Moses coming off the mountain. It sat on a hill of its own making, formed by decades of falling leaves and limbs. The height of the tree was so great that I had to lie on my back to fully appreciate this massive specimen. It was easy to lose track of time, laying there gazing through those massive tortuous limbs at the cerulean sky. Solomon, in all his glory, was not as regally attired as this sycamore. I was reminded of Joyce Kilmer's 1913 verse from his poem, "Trees": "Poems are made by fools like me but only God can make a tree." When I called my measurements in to the state forestry commission, it was the fourth largest sycamore recorded in Arkansas; the largest being on Crowley's Ridge.

Island transportation is by all-wheel drive vehicle or on foot. When it rains, the roads get very slick and soft. Stan employs an ancient military jeep that is ideal for this environment. On one occasion, his dysfunctional nose almost got us killed. In pitch black darkness we had loaded our guns and gears into his Hustler. He was just ready to fire it up when I said, "I smell gas." The floorboard and engine compartment were awash in gasoline-the fuel line had come loose. Had he turned the key, we would have been an integral part of a massive explosion–we almost joined the turkeys in the treetops.

One morning, the jeep battery was low and Stan opened the hood to jumpstart it. On the breather lay a very large rattlesnake. Thinking it was fake or dead and that he was the recipient of a prank, he called a friend over and said, "Take the breather off for me." Just as he started to comply, the snake moved, prompting a rapid reassessment of the situation. It took a while to remove that snake after it crawled under the motor. The reptile could just as easily have been under the front seat when Stan sat down to crank it. We now routinely inspect the vehicles before using.

One of the unwritten club rules is that you don't do what a bear does in the woods. The island ecosystem has its own botanical deterrent to discourage this practice. It's a plant locally known as rattlesnake weed. When it contacts bare flesh it causes a painful sting. I was introduced to this plant one morning when it became urgent that I break that rule. Not wanting to literally get caught with my pants down, I chose a patch of lush foliage and ducked into it. I thought at first I had intruded on a nest of yellow jackets or fire ants. Being a fast learner I soon deduced the cause of my pain. Some very sensitive areas were affected- I'll never forget that lesson!

The most memorable turkey hunt of my life played out on the island. We had crossed Mayhorn Bayou and had set our decoys at the junction of two logging roads. It was 10:30 a.m. and we had only seen a couple of hens. "Two big toms coming," Stan whispered, as he trained his binoculars. He called and soon had both birds coming, gobbling like crazy. Then, they hung up (wouldn't come any closer). They would walk away and come back, repeating this pattern half a dozen times. "Let's go." said Stan. "You're kidding?" I retorted. "They're not going to work. Let's go get lunch and try again in a couple of hours." Well, he's the expert, I thought. We slipped out quietly and I couldn't wait to get back. When we were out of earshot Stan explained, "We'll give those gobblers a chance to split up and all the hens will be on their nests. Then they'll be more likely to work."

After lunch we quietly returned and set up forty yards east of our morning location. Stan clucked once and a gobbler thundered back not a hundred yards to the west. "Get ready." he whispered as he quit calling. About one minute later the biggest gobbler I'd ever seen was hotfooting down the road. I waited until its head was behind a tree and raised my gun halfway. As he went behind a second tree I got my barrel all the way up and squeezed the trigger as his head appeared. He never kicked. It was a four-year-old with a twelve-inch beard and one and a quarter inch spurs. It was a real trophy and the pinnacle of my hunting experiences. His mount now hangs in my dental office.

It rains a lot on Big Island. On one hunt, with zero chance of rain in the forecast, it rained so hard that Stan and I had to get down on our hands and knees with downturned faces to keep from drowning. It felt like someone throwing buckets of water on your head. All that rain necessitates Thermacells and other bug-repelling measures.

A lot has changed on Big Island. Andreson-Tulley has harvested the tall pecan trees and the immense sycamore is no longer there. It was probably used to make pallets so the Chinese could ship their junk to your local Wal-Mart store. The flood of 2011 decimated the wildlife but it's making a comeback. The island barely escaped becoming part of a national refuge under the control of the federal government. That would have been worse than the great flood. Big Island has survived and is still the promised land of those who crave the ultimate wilderness experience.

Chapter 12

The Rattler

Let me preface this true story with the admission that I am not normal; normal is boring. I do things my way and I don't start something I can't finish. I am obsessively driven. I let nothing – romance, poverty, near-death experiences—interfere with my quest for success. I have experienced poverty and vowed to rise above it. I've hauled hay and cleared new ground in 100-degree heat. I've chopped and picked cotton until my hands bled. This was a powerful incentive to change my station in life. My late friend John Boyeskie once told me that I was "wound too tight and I needed to back off." I've always had the specter of poverty and fear of failure in my rearview mirror, pushing me even faster.

My work ethic was engrained at an early age – with a switch, belt, whatever was handy. I am the product of a strict, religious upbringing and didn't do pre-marital sex. I was taught to respect and honor women, not use them. I don't smoke, use drugs or drink to excess. I'm a registered organ donor, so someone will soon be getting some really clean, used body parts!

My college schedule and self-imposed expectations allowed little time for socializing. One of my most memorable dates was a nursing student named Marsha Joy. Her momma named her well. She was always smiling and cheerful. She was far too fine for this backwards country boy with limited social graces. I had no sooner picked her up from her dorm when she told the following joke: "What did Jackie Kennedy get Ari Onassis as a wedding gift?" Answer – "an erector set!" The prettiest girl I'd ever dated had just told a joke about erections! I began to sweat and my brain quit functioning so I changed the subject. I soon found that Marsha was delightful, sweet and intelligent and was a genuinely nice girl. I adored her and remember wishing I had the time and resources to properly court her. Sadly, I had neither—time and tides wait for no one.

Due to my exceptionally high grades, I was selected for early admission to dental school which would start in a few weeks. I had lots of soybeans to plant before classes began.

The pressure at U.T. Memphis dental school was intense; on a scale of 1-10 it was a 15. High stress sleep deprivation and an impossible workload all contributed to a prison-like atmosphere. During orientation the dean told us, "Look to your left. Now, look to your right. In one year one of you won't be here." Then he left the room. That was orientation.

My goal, of course, was to graduate first in my class so I would be eligible for a post-graduate residency. Fortunately, a few days break was scheduled between academic "quarters". It was during one such break that my life almost ended.

My usual Friday routine was to study and do lab work (crowns, dentures, etc.) until midnight, then head home to work on our Carlisle farm. I drove an old, green, push-button-shift Dodge® Polara that I'd purchased for $150.00. It didn't look like much but that sucker would fly! On its maiden run I'd surpassed 120 mph before the speedometer quit.

After midnight there were never any police between Memphis and Carlisle. I'd started accelerating midway over the Mississippi River bridge and would keep the pedal down. I didn't have a speedometer so I never knew how fast I was going. I made some very fast trips. I didn't have a death wish. I just had the "need for speed" and no time to waste. I never carried a passenger or endangered other drivers. I kept my guardian angel working overtime!

I once hit a dead bear on I-40 near Hazen, then the tailgate of an 18-wheeler that flew off in front of me. Both times, the car became airborne and landed in a shower of sparks. Fortunately I'd learned from the Dukes of Hazzard show that when you become airborne you accelerate to maintain control on impact. It works! After the bear strike, I checked the Dodge® for damage. There was none; it was built like a tank! There was just a lot of blood, hair and bear grease to clean off. What can I say? I was a redneck; now I'm an educated redneck!

On this particular Friday, I'd headed home early to do farm work. Police were everywhere, and since I had no speedometer, I drove with the traffic and got home at dusk. I quickly hugged my mom, donned shorts and sandals (mistake) and took my Lewellyn Setters for a much needed walk. It was dark when I returned to put them in their pen. They didn't want to enter (red flag) so I stepped in first. This careless lapse of woodsmanship cost me dearly!

I felt a sharp blow to my left foot that knocked me backwards into the fence. Then, I heard the rattler sound off and knew I was in trouble.

I fashioned a tourniquet from hay twine and hurried to the house. I got the snake-bite kit and razor and cut X's into the fang marks but couldn't get any venom out. Mother and I sped to the Stuttgart Hospital; a long and painful drive. My leg was on fire and swelling fast. It turned out that I'd done everything wrong, especially tying the tourniquet too tight.

When I reached the hospital, all hell broke loose. A stretcher was brought and I was whisked inside.

I was tachycardic, nauseated, sweating and in severe pain. IV's were placed and I was hooked to a heart monitor. No pain meds could be given.

When I stabilized I was taken to a room and my leg was packed in ice—all the way up! I worried that my reproductive function might be compromized, so I strategically insulated the family jewels from the ice. The ER doctor asked if I was sure it was a rattler. "Yes," I replied, "it rattled after it struck!" I was given antivenin and had a horrific night, shivering uncontrollably. The next morning I refused the Demerol and all pain meds brought thereafter. I didn't want to risk dependency. During my worst moments, I'd think of Marsha. That helped ease the pain. I remembered how beautiful she was in the moonlight at Cedar Point and how much I'd enjoyed the short time we had together.

My next brush with eternity occurred when I was given a tetanus shot. I began to itch, swell and couldn't breathe. I'd had an anaphylactic reaction to the tetanus. "You're damned if you do and damned if you don't." the doc opined.

My next conflict occurred when my pretty dark-haired nurse told me I'd need a catheter and bedpan. "No thanks," I said, "Give me those crutches." She unpacked the ice and I swung my leg off the bed, causing horrific pain. I passed out and hit the floor.

I awoke to her rubbing an iced towel on my face. "You're a pain in the a**" she remarked. "Are you ready for your catheter?" "Get me an orderly," I replied. When he arrived, I had him lift my swollen leg on to a wheeled stool then position me in another. I then propelled myself into the bathroom, using the crutches. The nurse mumbled something that I'm sure wasn't complimentary. I really didn't want that catheter! This became my routine for the next eight days and nights, with virtually no sleep, but I did it my way.

My only visitor, besides family, was a very pretty nurse named Melba Schafer. Against all odds, she would become my wife and give me two fine sons. She really brightened my day and gave me a little perspective.

I remember lying there in agony, wondering if I would lose my leg and if I could return to dental school. I thought at the time that my life couldn't possibly get any worse. Unfortunately, I was wrong. Watching my beautiful wife slowly die of Alzheimer's is infinitely more agonizing.

Upon discharge, my nurse told me why I got so much attention. A few weeks earlier a farmer from Gillett had been bitten by a cottonmouth and had died in the ER. I guess I was lucky after all.

Against doctor's orders, I returned to school three weeks later. I'd put my life on hold to get that degree and I needed to push on. My leg was still swollen, painful and looked horrible. To make it presentable I kept it neatly bandaged and pulled a sock over it. I had to get up early to get ready and make it to class where I would elevate my leg on an adjacent desk. The crutches made for slow going, especially on stairs. Several times one of the pretty hygiene students would offer to help, which I would politely decline. To this day I can't imagine why

I was so stupid! It was said that King James was the most educated fool in Christendom. I think that fits me precisely.

Shortly after I'd chucked the crutches I was walking across Forrest Park about midnight when two black boys decided to kill me with a gun. The first shot barely missed my left ear. I dropped to the ground and took evasive action as five more bullets kicked up dirt. I attribute their poor marksmanship to the fact they had never had to hunt for food. A country boy can survive! The gunfire brought lots of police and a helicopter. I'd gotten a good look at my assailants as they fled down Union Avenue. The officer wasn't interested in my report. He admonished me for being in the park after sundown, like it was my fault. How ironic and sad that those two black boys would try to murder a white boy while hiding behind the statue of Nathan Bedford Forrest, the former grand wizard of the KKK. I certainly bear those men no ill will but I sure am glad they missed!

About the time my leg returned to function I read Marsha's wedding announcement in the Memphis newspaper. She was marrying some guy named Skinner. I was truly happy for her. I'd chosen my path and had paid the price. After that I lowered my academic sights. I settled for being an honor graduate (top ten percent) and just trying to be a very good general dentist. I didn't even apply for the residency that had seemed so important. I had accumulated a huge debt and was mentally and physically exhausted and needed to "get a life".

I had started a promising relationship with a stewardess named
Beth but I killed that when I suffered a bout of post-partum
depression after graduation. I just stopped calling. I couldn't tol-
erate the lack of stress and was too ashamed to call her after I'd
snapped out of it. She certainly deserved an explanation.

Do I have regrets? Yes. Was my quest worth it? Yes. I've elimi-
nated a tremendous amount of pain and suffering and improved
the quality of life for thousands of people. My children and grandchildren will never know hardship. I'd built a luxurious house on
the Little Red River where Melba and I would relax between our
world travels. God had other plans. It now sits vacant and for sale.

In summary, I have been blessed beyond measure. Life has been
good-hard but good. I've learned that too much ambition can
be a curse. I have enjoyed the company of many good friends
and beautiful women-these are not mutually exclusive. Through
extensive biological studies I have explored the amazing com-
plexity and intricate interdependence of all living things. These
complexities are obviously not the result of time and chance, and
quite frankly make evolutionists look stupid. I know my days are
numbered. I have many more yesterdays than tomorrows. When
my time comes, I desire that my "parts" go to deserving recipi-
ents. The ladies to whom this book is dedication would certainly
get priority. I would be honored if my organ donation could pro-
long the life of any one of them.

At age sixty-seven, I still haven't slowed down. I've never mastered the art of relaxation. I practice dentistry three-and-a-half days a week and oversee my farms and properties. I have chosen to "run out the clock" on this earthly life by working and helping others. This also helps me cope with the progression of Melba's illness. Even though my life is currently a train wreck, my family, friends, faith and a little country music sustain me. I spend long days and nights caring for Melba. Her Alzheimer's has worsened. She needs twenty-four hour care including bathing, feeding and changing diapers. She no longer knows my name but deserves the best I can give her. I am honor-bound to care for her till death do us part. I don't start things I can't finish.

Dr. Jim Burleson

CPSIA information can be obtained at www.ICGtesting.com
Printed in the USA
LVOW08s0523201115

463384LV00001B/1/P